Spot's Fun Year

Eric Hill

Spot Goes to School

⭐

Spot Goes on Holiday

Spot Goes to School

Spot starts school today!

Good morning, Miss Bear.

Let's start with a little song.

What has Spot found inside the wendy house?

Look! Spot has made a word.

What did you bring to show us, Spot?

The playground is fun! Where's Spot?

It's time for

a story now, Spot.

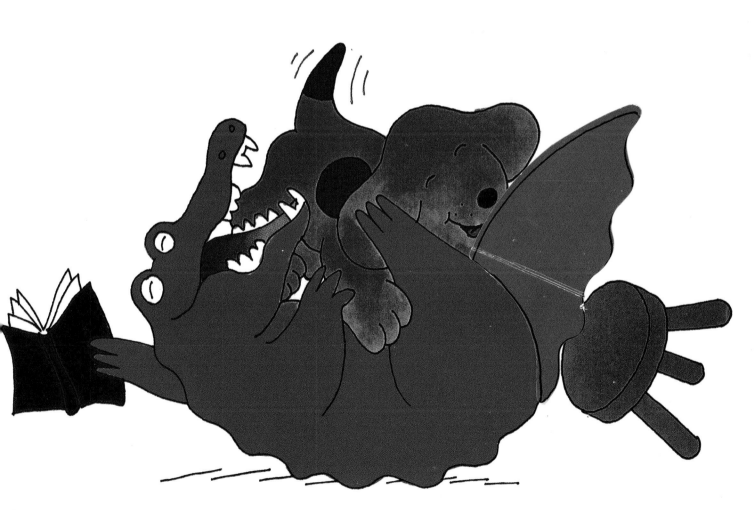

What's inside the blue box?

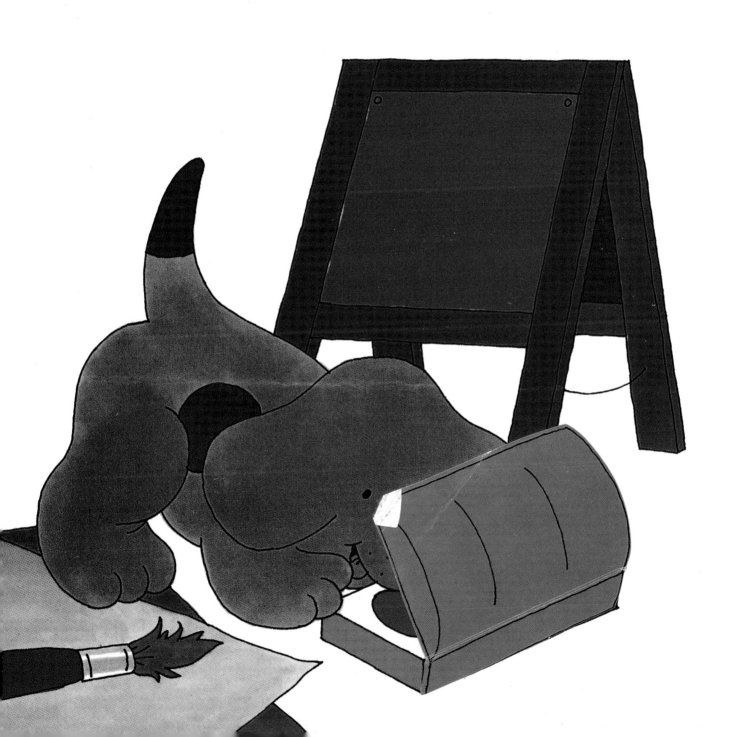

It's time
to go
home.

How was

Spot Goes
on Holiday

Dad and I

Spot wants to something.

buy

You really spoil

him, Sam!

Catch the ball,

Spot.

Sam is having a nap.

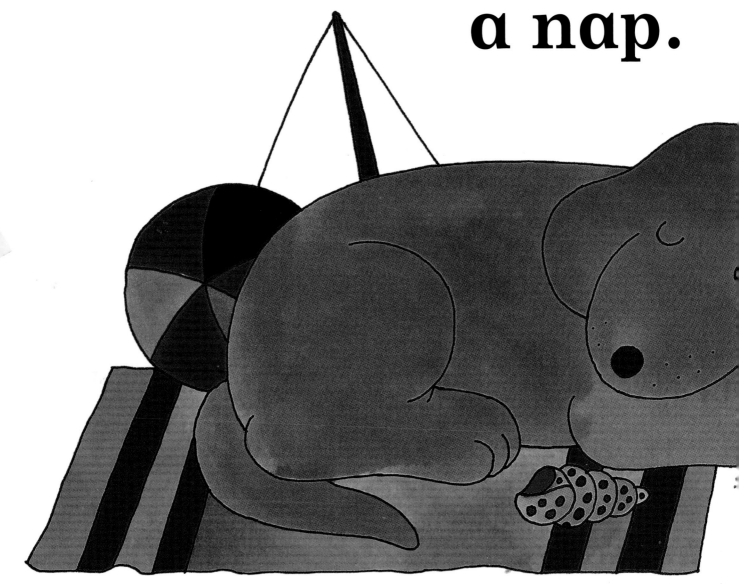

Where's Dad?

This is fun,
Spot.

Puppy

overboard!

Spot! That's not

What has Spot found now?

Come on, Spot.

You can play with your friend tomorrow.

Good!